A MINDSET PROGRAM

KNOW *your* WORTH

A WORKBOOK THAT
GUIDES YOU TO
STEP INTO YOUR
POWER AND OWN
WHO YOU ARE

BY ANTOINETTE &
RENEE BEAUCHAMP

COPYRIGHT © 2018 BY ANTOINETTE BEAUCHAMP
& RENEE BEAUCHAMP

ALL RIGHTS RESERVED. THIS BOOK OR ANY PORTION THEREOF MAY NOT BE REPRODUCED OR USED IN ANY MANNER WHATSOEVER WITHOUT THE EXPRESS WRITTEN PERMISSION OF THE AUTHORS EXCEPT FOR THE USE OF BRIEF QUOTATIONS IN A BOOK REVIEW. PRINTED IN THE UNITED STATES OF AMERICA

ISBN 978-0-578-43702-6

ONE & MANY[SM]

ONEANDMANY.CO | @ONEANDMANYOFFICIAL

DISCLAIMER: *client stories have been altered to respect client-coach confidentiality*

KNOW YOUR WORTH

ABOUT US

When we were teenagers, we weren't friends. We loved each other immensely, but we let outside forces get in the way – social pressures, clouded judgment, fear. It took Antoinette leaving home, a leap of faith, and our equally genuine desire to be close that brought us back together. Through tears, we made the choice to love and like each other because deep down we wanted to.

12 years later, we've written this workbook together. We went to college together, traveled the world together, cried over broken hearts together, and cried over love found together.

In 2016, our family's strength was tested when our dad was diagnosed with stage four colorectal cancer. It was devastating news and an even more devastating year of treatment. At the time, we lived together on the Upper East Side of New York City - Antoinette in fashion, Renee in media. Seeing the fragility of life, we started to question our lifestyle, values, choices, and career paths. We looked at everything through the lens of, "Is this really important? Does this matter? What difference does this make?"

In 2017, we both got laid off. It felt like the Universe opened the doors for us to step into something bigger, make an impact, and start our business together. We both moved to Florida after spending some time abroad and enrolled in yoga teacher training programs. Antoinette embraced the world of coaching and embarked on a journey to realize her calling of increasing consciousness in the world. Renee wanted more than ever to go deeper within and felt increasingly connected to everything that is wellness. Together, we crafted our business and dreamed of the lives we would change.

We started One & Many^{SM} to redefine personal development as global development. We want to inspire people to commit to their own work and healing so they can go into the world and share their light with others. In doing this, we shift and heal the collective consciousness. This world needs each of us to show up as our best selves, and we are dedicated to becoming better for each and every one of you.

Thank you for picking up this workbook and joining us on this mission. We love you. We send you love and light always.

LOVE,

Antoinette + Renee

DEDICATION

This workbook is dedicated to you, Mom and Dad. Without you we would not know what it means to love, live passionately, and go after what we want.

ACKNOWLEDGEMENTS

We are beyond grateful for the incredible humans in our lives that have supported us from Day One.

Thank you to our parents, you have always supported us, championed us, and encouraged us to take risks (still do).

Thank you to our brothers, who have always been our biggest fans and make us laugh. You make life better.

To our extended family, you know who you are. You have always had incredible faith in us, even when we abandoned our New York City careers to start a wellness business. We love you so much.

To our best and closest friends, thanks for keeping us real and cheering us on.

To our editor and brother, Michael Beauchamp, we are so proud of you. Thank you so much, this book would not be complete without you.

To our clients – your desire to change, your will to do the work and be vulnerable, and the leaps you have taken to look within has been everything. This book wouldn't even exist without you. You teach and inspire us every single day and we love you dearly.

To the authors and teachers that have inspired us along the way, you have taught us so much about yoga, coaching, and spirituality and inspired this workbook: our YTT teachers at Zeal Yoga and Breathe, Salt, & Yoga in Jupiter, Florida, IPEC Coaching Community, Michael Singer, Brené Brown, Debbie Ford, and Marianne Williamson.

To our coaches that have helped us with our own personal growth and development: Stacey Hartmann and Joseph Aldo.

To Alex, thank you for believing in me. Your love inspires me to be a better person. R

INTRO

KNOW YOUR WORTH: A MINDSET PROGRAM

INCREASE YOUR SELF-WORTH

We created this workbook to help shift your mindset to work *for* you, not *against* you. The exercises and lessons that follow will bring to light what has been holding you back and help you release what no longer serves you. Our goal is to help you recognize your worth and guide you into a more positive mindset so that you can create the life you want!

The concepts we'll explore are inspired by Core Energy Coaching™, yogic philosophies, and spiritual thought-leaders. We've consolidated these ideas with the most change-inducing topics we cover with clients in our coaching sessions to create a comprehensive program designed with your ultimate growth in mind!

The workbook has two parts and is intended to serve you for 14 weeks. If you let it, it will feed your soul for years to come.

Part 1 focuses on your healing. You start here to draw awareness to what you are holding onto or holding at bay because of your fears, anxieties, insecurities, and more. By bringing these to the surface, you'll be given the opportunity to let them go and move forward in your life. Part 2 prepares you to step into a new phase by reshaping the relationship you have with yourself to increase your self-worth.

PART 01
START YOUR HEALING

- 01 MINDFULNESS
- 02 ACCEPTANCE
- 03 TRIGGERS
- 04 SURRENDER
- 05 JUDGMENT
- 06 LIMITING BELIEFS
- 07 FORGIVENESS

PART 02
DEEPEN YOUR CONNECTION TO SELF

- 08 SELF-CARE
- 09 SELF-LOVE
- 10 INTUITION
- 11 VALUES
- 12 HOW YOU SHOW UP
- 13 VULNERABILITY
- 14 COLLECTIVE

This journey will be filled with shifts, ah-ha moments, and deep work to increase your energy, confidence, and level of fulfillment in your life. Believing in yourself is key to taking risks and making changes in your life. This journey will take you to the edge of your boundaries, so you can expand, fly, and take your life to the next level.

You are covering a lot of ground in a short period of time, so be patient and kind to yourself throughout the process. We feel so incredibly blessed to be on this journey with you and we are sending love and support from our souls to yours. You are on your path, enjoy every minute of it!

HERE ARE SOME TIPS TO GET THE MOST IMPACT AND GREATEST RESULTS OUT OF YOUR WORKBOOK:

- Find an accountability buddy (e.g. coach or inspiring friend) to check in with and support you along the way.

- You'll notice each week starts with a Sun Phase. The Sun is a symbol for starting anew, as each day is an opportunity for a fresh start! These sections shine light on the new topic for the week and work as thought-provokers and awareness builders. Each Sun Phase will have a key thought for you to hold on to throughout the week.

- Begin each Sun Phase on Sunday or Monday.

- Move into the Moon Phase at the mid-end of each week. The Moon represents reflection and a time to release. This is where the real work lies. This phase dives deep into how the topic you explored early in the week is manifesting in your life.

- Complete each Moon Phase before starting the next topic.

- Consider using the Sun Phases as a daily practice for a more intensive process. To do so, revisit the Sun Phase each morning of the week. This will keep it top of mind and allow awareness to form quicker.

- We recommend using this program in conjunction with private coaching. With private coaching you have a guide, cheerleader, and an incredible amount of accountability and support. Consider it a fast-track to creating the changes in your life that lead to better relationships, personal fulfillment, wealth, and more!

- Use the "Free Write" pages at the end of each section for your own journaling and free flow stream of consciousness!

FREE WRITE

Take time to reflect on where you are in your life right now. What made you purchase this workbook? What do you hope comes out of it? How worthy do you feel on a day to day basis? At your core?

_____

_____

_____

_____

_____

_____

_____

_____

_____

_____

_____

_____

_____

_____

_____

_____

_____

PART
01

START YOUR HEALING

Everyone has mental and emotional wounds from past and present experiences. These wounds aren't as obvious as most physical ailments, so many don't seek help to heal this suffering. Instead, you live with it, cherish it as part of who you are, and even protect it to avoid more pain – this is poisonous to your self-worth.

For the next seven weeks, we will guide you in unpacking some of these wounds. As you discover what has held you back, you'll not only be faced with the choice to let it go, but you will also notice that you do not need to define yourself by your experiences. You are more than what has happened to you and what you have done. Through this phase of releasing, you will clear space and shift your energy toward openness, love, and compassion.

Setting intentions and repeating affirmations are key to creating change. As you begin your healing process, we encourage you to center yourself and repeat the healing affirmation listed below as often as you need!

FIND A COMFORTABLE SEAT

Close your eyes. Connect with your breath. Take three long, deep breaths. In and out. Draw your attention to your heart. Feel into this physical and energetic space. Visualize your mental and emotional wounds as physical wounds on your heart and body. Send healing energy and breath to your heart center. Picture your wounds healing. Repeat, "I am healed" as many times as it feels right for you.

LET'S GET STARTED.

WEEK 01

START YOUR HEALING

PRACTICE MINDFULNESS

sun phase

Even though the word mindfulness feels like a massive 'buzz' word at the moment, it truly is the bedrock of enhancing growth and improving self-worth. Along this personal development journey, there will be setbacks, moments where you still say things you wish you didn't, and instances where you replay the same stories of your past. Mindfulness brings you back to the present. During those times that you inevitably veer off track, it returns you to your development and self-work journey. As we see clients evolve, the one thing that has become their absolute ally is awareness. The power of being able to identify what's happening with you is huge!

Building awareness is the first step towards transformation. Living mindfully means becoming the observer. It means listening as your mind goes off in a million directions, and noticing when your energy or mood shifts. It means being in tune with what is happening in your head, heart, and gut. It means seeing things clearly and watching how you and the world around you interact. Without judgment, without trying to shift anything, mindfulness is seeing and hearing your inner and outer Self.

This first week, the key thought will be yours to create. Be mindful of your desires. Set an intention of your own. Say it aloud each morning when you wake up. Put it out into the universe, but be sure to let go of any attachment to the outcome! E.g. "I am exploring my mind with curiosity, love, and compassion."

KEY THOUGHT OF THE WEEK: I AM _____

moon phase

As you continue to go about your week, see if you can catch the voice inside your head. There are a lot of names for this voice – ego, inner voice, inner peanut gallery – and you rely on it for guidance and clarity. Listen for this voice. The more you practice listening, the more you realize that its chatter is nonstop, and instead of being a force for guidance, it often undermines you and your self-worth. This voice is not you and you are not defined by its whims.

If you find it difficult to remember to listen for this voice, carve out a specific amount of time: one hour, one meeting, or even one shower. Set the intention to sit back and listen, and when your awareness gets caught in your mind's chatter, see if you can re-center yourself. Try to sit back again and just observe.

WEEK 01

What have you noticed this week when listening to your inner peanut gallery? What are his/her favorite topics?

_____
_____
_____
_____
_____
_____
_____

How does your inner peanut gallery help you?

_____
_____
_____
_____
_____
_____
_____

WEEK 01

How does your inner peanut gallery hurt you?

_____
_____
_____
_____
_____
_____
_____

When you quiet the mind in moments of peace or meditation, what do you feel connected to?

_____
_____
_____
_____
_____
_____
_____

WEEK 02

START YOUR HEALING

ACCEPT WHAT IS

sun phase

So often, our thoughts and ideas of how things are *supposed* to be create conflict with what is. Our families push our buttons, trains are late, weather forecasts are wrong, but instead of letting those things go, we give them the power to transform our moods and emotions.

In each moment, you have a choice. You can continue fighting what is (by complaining, feeling anxious, angry, upset, running the scenario over in your head, etc.), or choose to accept it and let it go. You can choose your mindset.

Take a few deep breaths. Ask yourself – do I want to give this power over my mood and my energy? If the answer is no, accept what happened and remind yourself that everything happens for a reason.

This week, recognize when you start to feel something rustle your feathers. Practice acceptance and be mindful of where your resistance is.

KEY THOUGHT OF THE WEEK: AM I RESISTING REALITY?

WEEK 02

moon phase

As your awareness increases throughout the course of this workbook, you'll start to notice more patterns and behaviors that you've had throughout your life. This work is extremely valuable and important, as awareness is the beginning of change. As you become aware of your patterns, mindsets, thoughts, and emotions, you have the power to change them. Accepting where you are is the beginning of a lifelong journey. Accept where you are now, without judging, or pushing, or wishing you were somewhere else.

What is an area of your life, an event, or a relationship that you have had trouble accepting?

_____
_____
_____
_____
_____
_____

WEEK 02

What is it about this event/relationship/situation that disturbs you?

_____
_____
_____
_____
_____
_____

What personal beliefs or judgments are you placing on this situation?

_____
_____
_____
_____
_____
_____

How much are these beliefs/judgments affecting your life?

_____
_____
_____
_____
_____
_____

WEEK 02

How would it feel to truly accept and embrace the reality of the situation?

_____
_____
_____
_____
_____
_____

What is one step you can take towards acceptance?

_____
_____
_____
_____
_____
_____

WEEK 03

START YOUR HEALING

IDENTIFY TRIGGERS

sun phase

After spending two weeks honing your self-awareness, you may watch yourself and notice how you act or respond when things come up in life. Noticing and taking responsibility for your reactions to others is particularly eye opening! As you move about your week, try to be super aware when anything disturbs you. Draw your attention to what's happening in your body, even before your peanut gallery starts to comment. Does your heart skip a beat, drop into your belly, or start to race? Does your stomach knot, drop into your butt, or otherwise churn? Your body reacts before your mind can create words to describe it. That's your subconscious at work trying to tell you something! These stomach-knot moments are what we call *triggers*.

As you watch your body this week, jot down any of these 'triggers' that you find, or just create a mental note. AND, hold gratitude in your heart for your body literally showing you what's energetically happening! Emotions = e-motions = energy in motion.

KEY THOUGHT OF THE WEEK:
I AM AWARE OF WHAT MY BODY AND ENERGY ARE TELLING ME.

WEEK 03

moon phase

What trigger(s) did your body show you this week?

_____
_____
_____
_____
_____
_____
_____

WEEK 03

Was there a thought pattern associated with this trigger? What was it?

EMOTION/FEELING IN THE BODY:

THOUGHT:

How might being aware of this pattern help you going forward?

_____
_____
_____
_____
_____
_____
_____

Now, show some gratitude to your body! What are 3 things you appreciate about your body and its abilities?

_____
_____
_____
_____
_____
_____
_____

WEEK 04

START YOUR HEALING

SURRENDER CONTROL

sun phase

For most people, controlling situations feels natural, but it is often driven by fear. Have you noticed the stress and unease that surfaces when you try to control a situation and don't get your desired outcome? Realizing you cannot control other people or outside forces can be incredibly anxiety inducing, but if you can push past the initial frustration, it can also be extremely liberating. We're here to offer one thing: freedom.

In a perfect world, everything would happen exactly how we want and when we want. While things do play out that way sometimes, it's not always how life works. One amazing superpower is knowing that no matter what happens in life and what feels out of control, you can control yourself and your reactions.

This week, can you empty your cup to make room for the unknown? Where can you surrender control? If you usually tell your spouse, kids, or co-workers how they "should" do things, can you sit back and let them handle it their own way? If you schedule yourself down to the minute in order to control how all your time is spent, can you free 15 minutes for nothing?

KEY THOUGHT OF THE WEEK: WHY DO I NEED TO CONTROL THIS?

WEEK 04

moon phase

The need to control is completely normal and affects most people. Whenever you feel the need to control a situation or person, it's helpful to look at *why*.

One of our clients, an entrepreneur with a lot on her plate, understandably felt the need to control everything around her out of fear that things would go 'wrong'. At work, she consistently micromanaged, mistrusted her employees, and had her hands in every area of her business. Her behavior not only affected her employees' morale, but it also impacted her energy at home. She would get irritated if things didn't go her way and uncomfortable when outside factors threatened her schedule.

During our coaching sessions, she revealed how chaotic and unorganized her home life was when she was young. We discussed how her demands for order and obedience are a reaction to that stressful experience. Because of her past, she built a life of rigid structure and control. Growing up, it was the only way for her to feel sane, but now it was impacting her business and everyday life. What she grew to understand is that her constant need for control doesn't help. It hurts. Now, she strives to be more open and accepting of change.

Surrender is the word.

WEEK 04

When it comes to your life, when does a need for control show up for you?

_____
_____
_____
_____
_____

What triggers your need for control?

_____
_____
_____
_____
_____

Was there a major stage or time in your life you felt out of control?

_____
_____
_____
_____
_____

WEEK 04

How connected are you still to that past time/stage in your life?

_____
_____
_____
_____
_____

What behaviors/patterns/beliefs have you adopted as a result?

_____
_____
_____
_____
_____

How can you release your need to control? What steps would you have to take?

_____
_____
_____
_____
_____

WEEK 05

START YOUR HEALING

RELEASE JUDGMENT

sun phase

It's completely understandable to judge experiences, people, and places based on your belief system and past, but judging puts your walls up. It keeps you separate and closed. It's a crutch to avoid self-criticism and point feelings of low self-worth in someone else's direction. With judgment, you are escaping your own pain and choosing to pick on someone else's. If we all released judgment and stood together in vulnerability instead of separation, imagine the impact on your life and others!

Healing yourself and releasing your own self-judgment will help bridge gaps and connections with loved ones and strangers alike. Keep this thought in mind as you go about your week and remember to be gentle and not judge yourself throughout the process.

KEY THOUGHT OF THE WEEK: WHAT I JUDGE IN OTHERS, I JUDGE IN MYSELF.

TIP: Use your notepad on your phone (or write an email to yourself!) to keep track of the "good" and "bad" judgments you're making about yourself and others. Labeling things as "good" is just as much of a judgment as labeling things as "bad".

WEEK 05

moon phase

GET CENTERED: Close your eyes, focus on your breathing, and connect with your heart in a calm, safe space. Reconnect with the thought of the week: "What I judge in others, I judge in myself". Replace judgment with love and acceptance, starting first with YOU.

The following questions are influenced by our reading of The Darkside of Light Chasers by the late Debbie Ford.

WRITE DOWN THE NAMES OF TWO PEOPLE YOU KNOW THAT HAVE QUALITIES THAT YOU ADORE AND ADMIRE. LIST THOSE QUALITIES:

_____

_____

Are these qualities you also see in yourself? _____

Do you strive to embody these qualities? _____

If your answers were yes, then here you see: what you see in others, you see in yourself!

WEEK 05

WRITE DOWN THE NAMES OF 2 PEOPLE YOU KNOW THAT HAVE QUALITIES THAT YOU DESPISE AND DISLIKE. LIST THOSE QUALITIES:

___

Are these qualities that you have expressed? If not, could you see yourself embodying these qualities if your life circumstances were different?

___

WEEK 05

Give an example of when you have embodied these qualities.
If you haven't, write down the circumstances under which you could embody them:

_____
_____
_____
_____
_____
_____
_____

How have you judged yourself or others when demonstrating these qualities?

_____
_____
_____
_____
_____
_____

By putting yourself in the Other's shoes and turning the pointer finger in your direction you see: what you judge in others, you judge in yourself.

WEEK 06

START YOUR HEALING

FREE YOURSELF OF LIMITING BELIEFS

sun phase

You hold a set of beliefs you've adopted or created throughout your life. These beliefs shape how you interact with the world around you – how you make decisions, perceive opportunities, and behave in relationships.

Low self-worth, resistance, and limitations in your life arise when you treat these thoughts as irrevocable truths. Taking inventory of the limiting beliefs you carry and impose on yourself is your first step in releasing them!

One of the most common limiting beliefs: I don't have enough time.

This week, start to listen to how often this comes up for you, whether you say it aloud or think it. Without judgment, bear witness and track how many times this belief comes up! Keep notes in your phone.

KEY THOUGHT OF THE WEEK: I HAVE ALL THE TIME IN THE WORLD.

* If there's another limiting belief that's a big pain point for you right now, feel free to explore that instead!

moon phase

You may hold limiting beliefs concerning money, time, love, relationships, work, family... anything! If you are feeling stagnant or held back in one of these areas, explore why you're stuck by writing out what beliefs might be contributing to or exacerbating that stagnation. For the purposes of this workbook, we'll stay focused on time.

"I don't have enough time"

This belief/thought is a product of a lack/scarcity mindset.
At our SXSW™ speech in March of 2018, we offered the audience a new perspective. Instead of telling yourself, "I don't have enough time", can you shift your mindset to one of abundance and instead say, "I have more than enough time"?

STEP 1: CHOOSE TO CHANGE YOUR MINDSET.
Even if it doesn't feel 100% real yet, tell yourself it is. In introducing new thought patterns, you're re-training your mind and eventually you'll start seeing a new reality that matches your new thinking. You have more than enough time. Tell yourself that your world is abundant. Say, "I have all the time in the world." Breathe. Affirm. Repeat.

STEP 2: BE PRESENT.
Be present in this moment. Not in the future or the past. Existing in the now expands time. When you are fully present, time feels as though it can last forever. Meditation is an amazing tool that brings you presence. It's a practice that slows you down and rewires the mind to re-center. Start a meditation practice, or get back into it!
Reminder: all you have is now.

WEEK 06

NOW, LET'S TAKE A CLOSER LOOK AT YOUR MINDSET. WE WILL START WITH TIME, BUT FEEL FREE TO APPLY THESE QUESTIONS TO OTHER LIMITING BELIEFS YOU MAY HAVE!

What is your current relationship with time now?

_____
_____
_____
_____
_____
_____

What would you say to time if it were a person? Is it a positive, loving relationship or a volatile one?

_____
_____
_____
_____
_____
_____

WEEK 06

How would you feel if you had all the time in the world?

_____
_____
_____
_____
_____
_____

What would you change your limiting belief to in order to support/serve you instead of hurt you?

_____
_____
_____
_____
_____
_____

In looking at how you spend your time now, where can you make space for what you really need/want in your life?

_____
_____
_____
_____
_____
_____

LIMITING BELIEFS

WEEK 07

START YOUR HEALING

FORGIVE YOURSELF

sun phase

Forgiving others is vital to personal growth and healing, however, giving that forgiveness to yourself is beyond powerful – it is transformational. Forgive yourself for your mistakes, judgments, and all the other self-imposed pressure you carry. By forgiving yourself, you invite love where there was pain. Light where there was dark.

We urge you to treat yourself with gentleness. Be gentle with yourself if you didn't make it to the gym before work this morning, or if you didn't respond to that work email. However big or small, keep an eye out for that moment to shine a gentle light onto your life and say to yourself, "It's okay, I forgive you."

As you practice forgiveness with the little things, consider forgiving yourself for the bigger life events that have happened.

KEY THOUGHT OF THE WEEK: I WILL BE GENTLE WITH MYSELF.

WEEK 07

moon phase

Think about all the negative self-talk you tell yourself. The limitations, judgments, and doubts you place on yourself when you're about to try something new or venture out of your comfort zone. These thoughts came from somewhere! They were not created overnight and the patterns have probably been there for a while. Part of forgiving yourself is finding the root cause and developing self-compassion for where it all began. It's time to forgive yourself for creating the negative self-talk, repeating it, and believing it.

I FORGIVE MYSELF FOR BELIEVING THAT I:

WHICH HAS BEEN HOLDING ME BACK FROM:

IT STARTED WHEN/CAME FROM:

AND INSTEAD I WANT TO TELL MYSELF:

WEEK 07

I FORGIVE MYSELF FOR BELIEVING THAT I:
_____
_____

WHICH HAS BEEN HOLDING ME BACK FROM:
_____
_____

IT STARTED WHEN/CAME FROM:
_____
_____

AND INSTEAD I WANT TO TELL MYSELF:
_____
_____

WEEK 07

I FORGIVE MYSELF FOR BELIEVING THAT I:
_____
_____

WHICH HAS BEEN HOLDING ME BACK FROM:
_____
_____

IT STARTED WHEN/CAME FROM:
_____
_____

AND INSTEAD I WANT TO TELL MYSELF:
_____
_____

You've heard the trusted saying, "Your thoughts create your reality." Paying attention to what you believe and tell yourself is an amazing technique that gives you the power to manifest what you want in this world. After forgiveness comes re-creation, and the opportunity to do and say things differently, to treat yourself with gentleness and improve your self-worth.

TIP: Use your new beliefs/thoughts as affirmations to repeat each morning you wake up! Choose high vibe words that are positive and make you feel inspired and motivated!

FREE WRITE

Reflect on this journey so far. What came up for you (ah-ha moments, triggers, breakthroughs, pain)? What has resonated with you most? What have you released since you started?

_____
_____
_____
_____
_____
_____
_____
_____
_____
_____
_____
_____
_____
_____
_____
_____
_____

CONGRATULATIONS!
YOU'VE COMPLETED THE FIRST HALF OF THE WORKBOOK!

Give yourself a hug and a huge pat on the back. Hopefully, regardless of what came up for you, you were able to release some things that may have been clouding your head and weighing down your heart. It's normal to feel the roller coaster of the self-development journey. One day you could be feeling on top of the world and the next you're crying on your bathroom floor. We get it!! And it's all totally normal!!

If you were particularly drawn to a certain topic over the past several weeks, we encourage you to follow your heart and explore more. Always feel free to reach out to us and ask questions on how to deepen your work and find greater healing. You are not alone on this journey. You are supported, and we love you. 💙

HOW OFTEN DO YOU CELEBRATE
YOURSELF? DO ONE THING
(AT LEAST!) THIS WEEK THAT
MAKES YOU FEEL SPECIAL!

PART 02

DEEPEN YOUR CONNECTION TO SELF

This second half of the workbook is all about connecting with *you*. Your relationship with yourself is the deepest, most fulfilling connection you'll nurture in your lifetime. You know the analogy about the oxygen mask? It's essential for survival. If you do not take care of yourself, it leaves you with little to nothing available for others. It's time to put your mask on first, and check in with yourself and your own well-being. It all starts with you. You deserve this deeper connection with yourself. It is necessary, and it will serve as the foundation to deepen your connection with others!

INTENTION OVER THE NEXT PART OF YOUR JOURNEY:

I am connecting with and honoring my authentic Self.

LET'S GET STARTED.

WEEK 08

DEEPEN YOUR CONNECTION TO SELF

PRIORITIZE SELF-CARE

sun phase

To improve your self-worth, you must dedicate time to yourself. Instead of seeing self-care as a luxury, try a different approach: It's non-negotiable! Think about what you want to get out of the time you spend with yourself. For example: Do you want to recharge, feel creatively inspired, or connect spiritually?

KEY THOUGHT OF THE WEEK: WHAT DOES SELF-CARE MEAN TO ME?

moon phase

How often do you practice self-care?

_____
_____
_____
_____
_____
_____

When practicing self-care, what do you want to walk away feeling?

_____
_____
_____
_____
_____
_____

WEEK 08

What do you say to yourself that keeps you from putting your needs first?

_____
_____
_____
_____
_____

What are some judgments you have around personal time and self-care?

_____
_____
_____
_____
_____

WEEK 08

What's another way to look at these judgments? Reference Week 6 to rewrite them as new beliefs.

_____
_____
_____
_____
_____
_____

SOME SELF-CARE PRACTICE TIPS:

- ◇ Yoga, meditation, set up a daily spiritual practice, free journal

- ◇ Color, paint, read, take some downtime and listen to music at home, dance in your living room

- ◇ Watch a show or movie, make dinner, go out to eat, have a glass of wine

- ◇ Take a bath, put on a mask, go to a spa

WEEK 09

DEEPEN YOUR CONNECTION TO SELF

LOVE YOURSELF

sun phase

Everything starts and ends with love in this world. Picture yourself when you were first born — a little beam of light, full of love and joy. You are still that same little being. We cannot express how important it is to reignite that flame of love from within. Infusing yourself with love is like pushing a large reset button. It recharges you. It allows for more vulnerability, connection, abundance, and infinite love!

Throughout your week, see if you can find moments to show yourself some love by treating yourself gently. If you find yourself engaging in negative self-talk, ask yourself if you would ever talk to the person you love most in the same way!

KEY THOUGHT OF THE WEEK: HOW CAN I HONOR MYSELF MORE TODAY?

WEEK 09

moon phase

What are three things you truly love most about yourself?

_____
_____
_____
_____
_____
_____

Send a text or call to four of your closest friends/family members and ask them what they love the most about you!

Combine these attributes into a list:

WEEK 09

TAKE YOUR WORKBOOK TO A MIRROR AND READ THE LIST ALOUD.

Then spend five minutes looking into your eyes. Not only is this a meditative experience, but by staring into your eyes you really start to see yourself beyond the body, beyond any masks – at a soul level. Tell yourself, "I love you". If you don't believe it, say it a few times. And know we love you, too!! Consider incorporating this as a daily practice for the remainder of the week (and however long you feel is right for you!).

Affirmations and mirror work do incredible things for your self-worth and energy levels. We had a client who was feeling a low level of self-esteem nearly every day. He was down in the dumps and putting himself down regularly. We had him focus on the positive qualities that he believed he had, plus the positive qualities others saw in him. We created daily affirmations that he read every morning when he woke up. Slowly but surely, his self-worth started to increase. He started seeing through a more positive, uplifting outlook instead of one that was bringing his energy down. Daily affirmations coupled with releasing old thought patterns and stagnant energy, helped him in a MAJOR way. We are huge proponents of positive self-talk and reminders of how wonderful you truly are!

WEEK 10

DEEPEN YOUR CONNECTION TO SELF

CONNECT WITH YOUR INTUITION

sun phase

People often ask, "what does your gut say?" That can be hard to answer if you can't tell your "gut" (intuition) from your inner peanut gallery or logical thinking mind for that matter. How can you learn to tell the difference?!

Your intuition = your Higher Self. So, if you were driving and needed directions, your Higher Self would be riding shotgun and helping you navigate with no hesitation or explanations. In contrast, your inner peanut gallery would have an upside-down map, be backseat driving and asking why you even bothered starting the car if you didn't know where you were going. You could have just taken a taxi.

How can you quiet this backseat driver to hear your Higher Self? Release self-doubt and rebuild self-trust. This is no small feat, and it may take longer to rebuild for some more than others. This week, check in on how connected you feel to your intuition. When you're faced with a decision, let your intuition guide you. Try the accompanied meditation to quiet the mind and get centered within. Meditation is a powerful technique to bring you into alignment with your Higher Self.

FIND A COMFORTABLE SEAT: Close your eyes. Connect with your breath. Take three long, deep breaths. In and out. Draw your attention to the crown of your head. Visualize yourself as your True, Highest Self, whatever that may look like. At the crown of your head is your Higher Self/Intuition, sitting in the driver's seat. Your loyal companion, your deepest level of wisdom. Imagine the light of the sun at the top of your head, extending through to your crown, feeding energy and power to your sense of inner wisdom. Picture your mind and body being connected with this Self, being guided by this Self. Keep breathing slowly and fully. Affirm: I am connected and guided by my Higher Wisdom. Repeat.

TIP: Fully read through the meditation before getting started. If it's challenging for you to remember the meditation, record yourself reading it aloud.

moon phase

Light a candle or make some tea and get comfortable before you journal below. Whatever gets you quiet and centered, whether you meditate beforehand or simply take a deep inhale and exhale a few times. Clear mind-space for your intuition to shine. Take your time to answer each question. If you have to come back to finish it another night, please do!

What does self-doubt feel like?
_____
_____
_____
_____
_____
_____

WEEK 10

Think back to when you were a child, when was the first time you remember feeling overwhelming self-doubt?

_____
_____
_____
_____
_____

How did you cope?

_____
_____
_____
_____
_____

If you could go back in time and speak to yourself at that time, what would you say?

_____
_____
_____
_____
_____

In what areas of your life does self-doubt come up for you today? Do you react in the same way that you did when you were young?

___

___

___

___

___

What is self-trust to you?

___

___

___

___

___

What is one step you can take towards rebuilding self-trust?

___

___

___

___

___

WEEK 11

DEEPEN YOUR CONNECTION TO SELF

LIVE TO YOUR VALUES

Being in tune with what you value opens the door to redefining priorities, creating goals, and understanding your joys and frustrations. Recognizing your values helps you live in tune with yourself, a key component of self-worth. Also, understanding your values can help you communicate more clearly with others. Going into the week, think about what you value and want to prioritize. Don't allow anyone else's "should" or outside influences affect what you hold as important in your heart.

sun phase

MAKE A LIST OF THE THINGS THAT GIVE YOU THE MOST JOY:

___
___
___
___
___
___
___
___
___
___

WEEK 11

From that list, what are the most important to you right now at this stage of your life?

_____
_____
_____
_____
_____
_____

From that list choose one as your key thought of the week. Try to live true to that value throughout the week and see how it manifests in your life. Notice how this impacts your feelings of self-worth throughout the week.

KEY THOUGHT OF THE WEEK:

moon phase

What discrepancies are there between how you live your life and the values you hold near your heart?

_____
_____
_____
_____
_____
_____

What do you want to prioritize differently?

_____
_____
_____
_____
_____
_____

What goals do you want to set? (2-3)

_____
_____
_____
_____
_____

WEEK 11

What's the first step you can take in the direction of your goals?

___

How soon will you start?

___

WEEK 12

DEEPEN YOUR CONNECTION TO SELF

CHOOSE HOW YOU SHOW UP

sun phase

As we discussed in Week 9, you are pure love at your core. Throughout your life, you have developed certain personas based on your environments, your upbringing/family, and so much more. Every situation has left an impression on you and helped mold you into who you are today. Of those personas, however, you've consciously or unconsciously decided to create certain masks that cover parts of yourself that are in your true nature. Have you ever had someone tell you that you were a completely different person in one scenario vs. another?

THINK ABOUT THESE QUESTIONS:

Is there any difference between who you are in front of a stranger, a friend, and a family member?
If yes, what are the differences?

_____
_____
_____
_____
_____
_____
_____
_____

WEEK 12

This week, do your best to recognize instances where you aren't living true to your nature and course correct. These moments are usually accompanied by a physical sensation, so be sure to draw on the awareness built over the course of Part 1 to understand when you are in such an instance.

KEY THOUGHT OF THE WEEK: I WILL BE MY AUTHENTIC SELF, NO MATTER THE SITUATION I AM IN.

moon phase

Time to reflect. Strengthening awareness around your moods and personalities is a major step, no matter how small the progress may seem now.

WEEK 12

TRY THIS EXERCISE: Reflect on how you currently show up in each situation and how you would like to show up by filling in this chart.

	NOW	VISION
work		
family		
friends		

WEEK 12

Take it a step further, and let's bring potential limiting beliefs to the surface.
Fill in the blanks:

Example: "My natural tendency to be _goofy_ at home is not good enough. In order to be _accepted at work___, I must _be more reserved and quiet__."

MY NATURAL TENDENCY TO BE _____

IS NOT GOOD ENOUGH. IN ORDER TO BE, _____

I MUST BE _____

MY NATURAL TENDENCY TO BE _____

IS NOT GOOD ENOUGH. IN ORDER TO BE, _____

I MUST BE _____

MY NATURAL TENDENCY TO BE _____

IS NOT GOOD ENOUGH. IN ORDER TO BE, _____

I MUST BE _____

WEEK 13

DEEPEN YOUR CONNECTION TO SELF

STAY OPEN

sun phase

"VULNERABILITY SOUNDS LIKE TRUTH AND FEELS LIKE COURAGE. TRUTH AND COURAGE AREN'T ALWAYS COMFORTABLE, BUT THEY'RE NEVER WEAKNESS."

Brené Brown, Daring Greatly

WEEK 13

It is completely natural to shut down, withdraw, or get angry in order to protect your heart from feeling pain. Protection mechanisms are formed instantly – often during childhood – to avoid getting hurt because it's easier to build walls, fortresses, and moats to stay safe and, ultimately, stay solo. It's time for a new age, where we (as a collective) can be raw with each other, where "flaws" and pain are celebrated as opportunities to do the work. Be willing to stay open no matter what!

This week, start looking for what your version of closing off looks like. You might silence yourself or physically remove yourself from a person or situation. You might dig in and fight. The outcome is all the same. The energy is all the same. When you're avoiding and fighting, you're reacting to what you view as assaults on your self-esteem or self-worth. When something bothers you, how do you react? Feel what happens in your heart. Try not to get swept away by what your mind tells you. *(Concept inspired by Michael Singer's The Untethered Soul)*

KEY THOUGHT OF THE WEEK: IS THIS WORTH CLOSING MY HEART OVER?

moon phase

CHECKING IN: recall a recent inner disturbance – a time when your inner peace was shaken (and you could have multiple).

What triggered you?

_____
_____
_____
_____
_____
_____
_____
_____

How did you react?

_____
_____
_____
_____
_____
_____
_____
_____

WEEK 13

What could you have done differently to respond with openness and vulnerability?

_____
_____
_____
_____
_____
_____
_____
_____

What can you tell yourself next time something like this comes up to remind you to stay open?

_____
_____
_____
_____
_____
_____
_____
_____

WEEK 14

DEEPEN YOUR CONNECTION TO SELF

SEE THE WHOLE

sun phase

One of your biggest opportunities for growth and healing is embracing the yogi view: **We are all one.**

Despite having technological capabilities that can seamlessly connect people around the world, we live separate and siloed lives. When we separate from each other and our true nature of love and harmony, we let anger, resentment, jealousy, and fear cloud our vision and lead our interactions. Let's change that pattern. Welcome and embrace each other, not as competitors or potential enemies, but as true friends. How do we treat our true friends? With love and compassion.

Last week, you chose to stay open. This week, put that into practice by looking at the people you pass. Everyone is trying to find their path, to care for their loved ones, and navigate the same demands of life that you are. Look at the people all around you and SEE them. SEE your likeness in strangers. Look into their eyes. Can you see their worth? Can you see yours reflected in it? Can you see that they are the same as you?

KEY THOUGHT OF THE WEEK: WE ARE ALL THE SAME.

moon phase

AFTER YOUR EXPERIENCE WITH THE SUN PHASE EXERCISE:

How did it feel to view strangers as equals? Any ah-hah moments or thoughts?

_____
_____
_____
_____
_____
_____
_____
_____
_____
_____
_____
_____
_____

How much do you believe that we are truly all one?

___

What do you like about this mindset? Dislike about this mindset?

___

WEEK 14

How could adopting this mindset serve you at this time in your life?

_____
_____
_____
_____
_____
_____
_____
_____

As you're exploring the energy of humanity, take some time to connect with the Earth. We are all made of the same elements and energy that formed this planet. Connecting with nature and the life-force energy within reconnects us with our true origins and allows for tremendous healing! So, whether you live in the city or country, find a space where you can place your hands on the earth. Touch the grass, sand, or snow. Meditate, take a walk, or practice yoga outdoors to get you connected to your environment. Breathe. Imagine your energy being drawn to the core of the earth. Get grounded!

FINAL

YAY!!!

CONGRATULATIONS!

You've completed 14 weeks of intensive self-work and healing to improve your self-worth! How has your mindset changed? What has changed in your life?

_____
_____
_____
_____
_____
_____
_____
_____
_____
_____
_____

What weeks have been the most intense/thought provoking for you? What exercises do you want to do more of?

_____
_____
_____
_____
_____
_____
_____
_____
_____
_____
_____

This is a great place to check in, go back and review how far you've come, what you want to continue to work on, and what intentions you have for the rest of your journey!

Now, reflect on this process and take a few minutes to rank the below.

Circle the number below that represents your current level of satisfaction in each area of your life!
(10 being perfectly satisfied, 1 being not satisfied at all)

INNER PEACE 1 2 3 4 5 6 7 8 9 10

SELF-LOVE 1 2 3 4 5 6 7 8 9 10

CONNECTION TO INTUITION 1 2 3 4 5 6 7 8 9 10

FULFILLMENT 1 2 3 4 5 6 7 8 9 10

LIVING TO YOUR VALUES 1 2 3 4 5 6 7 8 9 10

SELF-CARE 1 2 3 4 5 6 7 8 9 10

SELF-WORTH 1 2 3 4 5 6 7 8 9 10

FINAL

What would you have to do to improve each category by one point?

INNER PEACE
_____
_____

SELF-LOVE
_____
_____

CONNECTION TO INTUITION
_____
_____

FULFILLMENT
_____
_____

LIVING TO YOUR VALUES
_____
_____

SELF-CARE
_____
_____

SELF-WORTH
_____
_____

Finishing this workbook is a HUGE step in your growth and personal development journey.

Give yourself love and gratitude for seeing this through! It won't end here and honestly, we're not sure it ever ends! But the commitment you have made to yourself in completing this program, says so much about your power and ability to change. The awareness you've gained is life-changing. It cannot be undone or forgotten.

We hope you're feeling connected and empowered to go out into the world to share your light! You are a being of tremendous value. Come back to the work you've done here and dive further in the areas you need. There are so many resources available to do this work either with the help of a coach, a spiritual teacher or through solo study/practice. If you're looking for long-lasting, sustainable change, we encourage you to take a leap and explore private coaching!

We love you and we are here to support you on this path.

WITH LOVE AND LIGHT,

Antoinette + Renee

FREE WRITE

Additional space for journaling reflection and notes. Write your heart out!

Made in the
USA
Columbia, SC